A HEART FULL OF PRAYERS

PASTOR PEARL MOSES

authorHOUSE®

AuthorHouse™ UK
1663 Liberty Drive
Bloomington, IN 47403 USA
www.authorhouse.co.uk
Phone: 0800 047 8203 (Domestic TFN)
*   +44 1908 723714 (International)*

Published by AuthorHouse 07/05/2019

ISBN: 978-1-7283-8972-1 (sc)
ISBN: 978-1-7283-8973-8 (e)

Print information available on the last page.

CONTENTS

Part 2–A Heart Inspired

ENDORSEMENTS

The value of a book to me is determined largely by the life of the author. In Pearl we have a woman of God, a woman who displays true hunger for God and points the way for others to follow. I read this book with tears streaming down my face - tears of joy because of the intimacy it invites me to and tears of pain as it grapples with the complexities of life. This book will not be a quick, one-off read but something to return to and something that will help us all draw near to our Father.

Pastor Alistair Taylor

My personal interactions with Pastor Pearl Moses in her early Monday morning devotions has led me into her world of bible based, intercession.

Pastor Pearl Moses has poured out herself in this book of prayers in a way that engages with everyday life. Her beautiful prayers are deep and poignant, and are anchored in the word of God. In this collection of prayers, her ministry shines forth beautifully and helps us all connect with scripture and our hearts cry.

This book will help every one focus on important truths in the word and bring focus to our prayers. A powerful tool for strengthening prayer time, I am delighted to recommend this to all.

Omolara Cookey
Artist. Blogger. Award winning
entrepreneur. Motivator.

Somethings in life go together so easily, like strawberries and cream or salt and pepper. Then there's Pearl and prayer; it's hard to think of a more naturally supernatural pairing.

It's said that children, as they grow, learn to pick up on phrases and characteristics of their parents. Before long they may even sound the same, act the same; reflecting their parents in so many ways. Pearl's prayers are a reflection on her Father- her Heavenly Father. They are born of his character, his heart, his thoughts. She has the Father's heart and the Father has hers.

Each prayer takes you directly to the Father's heart, pausing to look at the world through his eyes as they lift you into his presence. Prayers for grown ups that bring a childlike freedom. This book gives you permission to throw caution to the wind and run headlong into the arms of the Father, knowing that is the best place to be. And it's from that vantage point that Pearl helps us to cry out to him. A place where we can see our hurts, our needs and the needs of others much more clearly; from God's perspective. A gem of a book to cherish, meditate on and revisit.

Alison Morley
www.downrightjoy.com
04/06/2019

Pastor Pearl Moses's prayers have been a blessing to many people over the years. This book is no exception. It expresses the real, day to day emotions we so often feel alongside a genuine intimacy with Father God. The result is prayers that will inspire and move the hearts of both those who are just beginning to pray, as well as the most passionate prayer warrior. Pearl's prayers are so authentic, so heartfelt, it is almost like being given the privilege of sitting beside her in her devotional times, to learn from one of the masters. When people say that prayer is hard, or boring, or it has become about getting from God, not giving to him, a 'have to' at the end of the day, or a last resort when facing trouble, may this book remind us of the way God meant prayer to be. The prayers are so rich with love, beauty and truth, so deep and wide, they are a delight to be savoured. I am sure all who read them will be encouraged in their primary purpose – to know and be known by our incredible God.

Beth Moran
Writer & Speaker
https://www.bethmoran.org/

Breathe in prayer breathe out prayer that's what I was doing rhythmically one evening as I went for a fast paced walk.

I found each step I took was becoming more purposeful and focused.

I had just stumbled across the breathing prayer and it seemed powerful but I wanted to make sure I was 'safe' so I called my 'phone a friend' Pearl, our trusted prayer warrior and asked her ' Pearl have you ever heard of breathing prayer?'

'Oh yes of course' came her knowledgeable and confident reply 'it's an old and established prayer method '.

I was not surprised that Pearl was familiar with my new prayer discovery and I was comforted that I wasn't straying into some strange territory.

This is who Pearl is to me - the person who deeply loves God and who understands prayer, so I recommend Pearl and I recommend Pearl's prayer anthology wholeheartedly ... I am convinced this compilation will have a lasting and positive impact on all who read it.

Usibakaiye Agbeyegbe

A Heart Full of Prayer. Reading through the manuscript, We are undoubtedly drawn to the Words: A HEART FULL... Indeed a practical prayer journal for every believer; Leaders and lay men alike with hearts are full from times of intimacy with Abba Father. This journal makes us know that it is possible to be a person of Prayer as it captures all vital areas of life and living. Worshippers, Intercessors and all in the Pulpit Ministry should read this book and probably use it as a Local Assembly's Prayer Journal. As Worship Warriors, we are so blessed to be able to have such a journal to heighten personal times of Worship and Intercession. Indeed, our hearts are full.

Pastor Patrick and Princess Pat Mohie.

"Everyone should pray, but not all pray and not all who pray have been gifted with the spirit of grace and supplication. I have discovered that those who the Lord has gifted with the grace of intercession are able to help others cultivate and develop deeply passionate and meaningful prayer lives. Pastor Pearl is one of those leaders with the grace to lead others in prayer as well as kindle the fire of prayer in their hearts. I have had the privilege of observing Pastor Pearl's passion for the Lord in the place of prayer, as a Mary contented to 'sit at His feet' and listen to the burden of His heart. Pearl was a regular member of the All Night Prayer Meetings at the LCC Tabernacle at North Acton, London in the late 90's. They were nights of incredible grace in intercession and Pastor Pearl's contribution is recorded in glory. I am so delighted that she has now captured some of her heart in print and I have no doubt that the Lord will use this book on prayer to ignite and renew your passion for prayer and intercession. A Heart Full of Prayers covers a range of intercessory burdens that are vital for these days. Like it has been said the future belongs to the intercessor and I ask you to shape the future and destiny of our nations and its peoples with your intercession. Follow Pastor Pearl as she helps you catch the burden and heart of our Lord and Saviour Jesus Christ!

Pastor Charles Abraham

The first words uttered when I was asked to write a few Words for this Book were .. "What an Honour!" The synonyms - 'Privilege', 'Awesome Pleasure' followed in quick succession, as with each page turned, I unwrapped this Beautiful Treasure; a literal Call to the unashamed, unhindered Worship of our Audience of ONE!

With pure (raw) unadulterated Worship poured out in a ceaseless flow from a yearning heart (like the woman with the Alabaster Box), Pearl inspires the same in us. "This Book" not only seeks to lead the 'Older' Believer into more intimacy with our Lord (a self-revival of sorts); but also provides a 'firm helping hand' to the 'New' Believer as he or she navigates the Journey of Salvation; discovering at each junction that Salvation is not an Event, but a life-long commitment grounded in true Worship. John 4.23.

"This Book" is a delightful read and the references to the ordinary, everyday occurrences are so easy to relate to that, the One who is yet to believe, would be stirred; intrigued by such revelations of our intimate relationship with our ABBA Father and the professed love of our God!

Even as Pearl prays for the different People Groups and Issues, her passion is as unwavering as her Faith in the Only ONE who hears and answers Prayers. Again and again, she appeals to us to have compassion, to intercede and take whatever steps to make the required difference; wherever we can.

This is such an exquisite write up on Worship which nudges us into the sweet fragrance of HIS presence and .. so much more, as we serenade HIM; putting us in the cherished position to receive of HIM. Mth 6.33.

I cannot commend it enough!

May God bless you Dear and; all whose great fortune it is to read 'this Book'. Amen

Omolara Akinola (nee Awesu)
Friend; Classmate, so many years ago

"Pastor Pearl Moses has captured a heart walk of prayers with her beloved Lord and written a must-read primer for anyone on a journey to deeper intimacy with our King. Read this book - and be inspired to pray as naturally as you breathe" —

H Michelle Johnson,
Author of Do Great Exploits, Speaker and Radio Host
www.hmichellejohnson.com

"A delightful guide full of insightful information for those of us who want to enjoy day-to-day fellowship with our beloved Heavenly Father." —

Pastor Kayode Pitan, Assistant Regional
Pastor, RCCG Region 20.
MD/CEO Bank of Industry, Nigeria.

This book of prayers has been a long time in the making and I am gratified that the Lord has brought it to fruition. It is truly inspired by the Holy Spirit and will challenge you to deepen your walk with God through prayer. I was blessed beyond measure and challenged to seek greater intimacy with the Lord. I believe that all who read it will be richly blessed.

Bola Soyannwo

"I've known Pearl for quite a while now, and whenever I spend time with her, I feel as though I have also spent time in God's presence. Her words often naturally weave between her conversation with you and her communion with the Father in heaven. She cultivates His presence wherever she goes, she prays as naturally as she breathes, and she deposits His wisdom and grace to everybody she encounters. And so, it is no surprise to me that this beautifully inspired book is actually an invitation into intimacy with the God that Pearl knows so well.

Of course, like every believer, I love to pray, but it's sometimes hard to find the right words. It helps me enormously to read prayers that put vocabulary around the thoughts and feelings I long to express, but often don't know how to. With her trademark quirky humour, honesty and deep reverence for her Saviour, Pearl has crafted prayers, readings and responses that resound with truth and love. I can already see how these would translate into many places, from quiet times to gathered meetings, creating a posture of prayer and connecting people with the heart of God.

Genuinely, I am thankful for all Pearl has modelled to me about living a life of holy but simple intimacy with Jesus. And I am also thankful that finally we have this resource of riches to read and re-visit again. Pearl, it really was worth the wait. I believe and I pray it will be a blessing to many."

Cathy Madavan,
Speaker, Writer, Coach and author of
Digging for Diamonds and Living on Purpose
http://cathymadavan.com

"I have known Pearl for nearly 10 years and been blessed by praying with her regularly in that time. This book captures her voice and her heart of passion and intimacy with her dearly beloved Lord, and it is a blessing and a provocation to be invited into her prayer space and to dwell with God there alongside her.

As you read, and worship, and pray your way through this journal you can sense that this life of prayer is just like the breath of life for Pearl. As you wrestle with her through the ups and downs of life, this journal offers opportunities to engage with Scripture and with God yourself and to pour out your own heart and prayers. I encourage you wholeheartedly to take up this gift."

Revd Jo Pestell, Trustee of Free Range
Chicks and Vicar of St. Catharine's Gloucester

"Pearl Ola-Moses is a Wordsmith. She loves words and is happy to be in world where words are crafted, after all she grew up around books and from an early age was encouraged to read and found her love for words.

Then Pearl grew up, I meet her in search of The WORD we became friends. We shared a common love for the WORD. I had the honour of being her Pastor (shared joy and responsibility with my late husband Alfred).

Today Pearl and I still get excited, in fact giddy over the discovery of another author, a book and a story that we can share together. . . it is not unusual to get a phone call just to ask if I read a particular

sentence and what are my thoughts. Pearl would chuckle and say '...you get it' by inference she is simply saying "you get me and my love for words"

Pearl has written a book "A Heart full of Prayers" an invitation to a private conversation gone public- you and I now have permission and access in the hope that the conversation, prayers and musing may even inspire our own search for the WORD. . . and hear HIM"

Abby 'the Vicar' Olufeyimi
Surrey
England

A HEART FULL
OF PRAYERS

My prayer for you is that prayer becomes as natural to you as breathing.

A Heart Full of Prayers is a communion with God journal by Pastor Pearl Moses. The journal chronicles reflections, musings, and prayers to inspire readers to greater intimacy and fellowship with our loving Abba Father in prayer.

In part one, each section is a snapshot of devotional thoughts on a topic, including prayers and scriptures, to serve as a springboard for the reader's own prayerful conversations with the Lord.

Part two is a selection of inspirational prayers often prayerfully written in the moment in response to situations, readings, or events. My heart is that these prayers inspire you to capture your own prayers too.

A Heart Full of Prayers is offered in love to prayer people and worshippers everywhere. It's a love primer for kingdom children who simply want to hang out with their heavenly king and beloved Lord.

> And Enoch walked with God; and he was not, for God took him. (Genesis 5:24 NKJV)

SOLI DEO GLORIA

(Inspired by UCB word for today based on a devotion about Bach)

Dear Lord, I read in a UCB Word for Today devotional that Bach started every music score with the words JJ—Jesu, Juya, 'Jesus, help me'. At the top and at the bottom of every composition, he inscribed three letters, SDG, for Soli Deo Gloria—'to the glory of God alone'.

These words moved me deeply, Father, because it's taken me years to get this book out, wrestling often and wondering whether it would be good enough.

Good enough for the world, good enough for a publisher, good enough for unknown and unnamed critics somewhere out there.

Wondering, would it pass muster? Would it make the grade? And so time after time, I'd start writing, then lose confidence and stop, and start over and over again.

And each time I stopped, I'd tell myself that perhaps it was presumptuous to think that I could write a book.

Yet, Father, slowly and surely the words kept coming.
Faith grew within me, and the prayers bubbled up and kept overflowing.

And as they did deep inside me, I knew that this book of our words had to exist.
Had to come forth and live outside of my heart.
Had to live in the world in any way You choose.

So, dearest Lord,
Here's this work of my heart …

For Your glory alone, Lord,
Acknowledging how great Thou art.

A work for Your eyes,
The audience of one.
A love gift,
An offering,
A sacrifice done.

So I no longer ask,
Is this book good enough?
Instead I present it to You, Abba Father,
Straight from my heart.

SDG

THANKSGIVING, THANK-YOUS, DEDICATIONS, AND MEMORIALS

With thanks to and adoration of my breath-taking-away, heavenly Abba Father.

Precious Lord Jesus, take all the honour and glory for the inspiration to write.

I'm humbled by Your mercy, Lord, as You continually draw me closer to You.

Sweet Holy Spirit, I'm forever grateful for Your presence, Your tenderness, and Your care.

You are my everything, my all in all.

Every vision needs friends, cheerleaders, supporters, life givers, destiny helpers, and co-incubators who come alongside and believe in it. In addition, to come forth alive, the vision also needs inspirers and disciplinarians, strong ones unafraid to push the vision carrier until the vision manifests.

This prayer journal would never have been written without some very special people. Each name below represents a life that intersected (and still does) with mine at key moments and in doing so stoked the fire of prayer and writing within me.

To every single one of you, I give my heartfelt thanks, respect, and love. I dedicate this book to you.

- ❖ My very special husband and man of God, Ola Moses. Babes, thank you for a lifetime of prayers, cups of tea, 'cheeks', smiles, and the rocksteady assurances that one day I'd write books. I love you deeply and always.
- ❖ Dear Pa and Ma (Prof and Chief Mrs Gladys Uche Uko Uche), my parents, faithful people of God and lovers of words and books: thank you for all your sacrifices and care. I know that my love of words and books came from you both, along with so many, many other things.
- ❖ Beloved Rev Betty King, prophetess, teacher, and great woman of God. My mentor who has fought for me, determinedly believed in me against the odds, and prayed for, challenged, promoted, and disciplined me long enough in ministry to see this book come forth. Beloved Rev I am truly grateful to you. May all your children continually arise and call you blessed.

❖ My dear Sibbies, sisters Ola, Ije, and AnGee and brothers Doc Chidi, Uzomba, and Tim: you are blessings directly from heaven. Each of you is a unique treasure, and it's awesome to see God's work unfolding in your lives. May God continue to smile on you and be gracious to you always.

❖ My lifelong friends, sisters of the heart, Gerri (the Miah), Bimbo (Atim), Jade, Siba (Sibaling,) Ayotola, Bola O (Bolibred), Njideka (Njitikins), Michelle, and Marylyn: thank you for all the times of sisterly prayer and sharing over the years. I believe we've shifted more in prayer than we will ever truly know while still down here on earth.

❖ Pastor Abby Olufeyimi, dearest pastor of my heart, woman of precious intimacy with Abba Father. Mere words can't do your part in my life's walk justice. And even so, these phrases mean so much. Thank you for 'Still Waters', carrot cake, Oluwaditton croft refuges, shekere high praise, and "The Lord" moments... I know you understand.

❖ Pastors Femi and Kayode Pitan, people of God and titans of faith: you are such inspirations to me and many others. Thank you for years of ongoing friendship, encouragement, prayers, and support.

❖ To my dear friends from FRC: Jo, Beth, Vicky W, Jude, Julia (QB), Fiona and Alison. Your love, care and compassion mean the world to me. Thank you for your deep, spirited friendship.

❖ Mary Stretch, dear woman of God: without those hidden oasis days at your place in 'Brentwood', this book might not have been completed. Thank you for your hospitality, my friend.

❖ Princess Min M: your 'diamond' gift challenged me to 'just keep on writing'. Thank you again, and may you always walk among people who will believe in your dreams.

❖ Dear Liz Sheik, thank you for everything; you are so good at what you do. Your words gave me a missing piece of the jigsaw. Thank you, my friend.

❖ Sheila C, for deep words and compassion that helped me broker so many ways through when it mattered the most. Thank you, woman of God.

❖ Truth Vine Church: wow, family, what can I say? You are simply the best. Dear pastors and leaders, you are the real deal. Men and women of fire and the Spirit, thank you for the privilege of serving God together.

❖ To every niece, nephew, and young person who calls me Aunty: I love you all and believe in you completely. Do exploits, for you are destined for greatness. I am praying for you.

AND IN LOVING MEMORY OF:

Pastor Alfred Olufeyimi, who encouraged me to pursue Abba Father in the Most Holy place above all else I might ever do in my Christian walk.

Sister Mercy Ohewere, who first modelled deep, fiery love for Jesus and fervent passion for His word to me so many years ago.

Vicky Taylor, my dear, dear friend and covenant sister. Forever loved; never forgotten. Vicky, I know you are having a ball with Jesus in heaven. Here's that book at last!

Pastor Pearl Moses
April 2019

PART ONE

A HEART FULL

PRAYER AS NATURAL AS BREATHING

My prayer for you is that prayer becomes as natural to you as breathing.

Precious Abba Father, I don't remember when I first realised just how vital prayer is to me—how unutterably precious and life-sustaining it had become simply knowing You are always there. Father, You know that I couldn't say I'd morphed into a towering prayer giant or champion intercessor, yet somehow, somewhere along the line, a shift had taken place, and I recognised this pressing desire to commune with the divine, this thirst to talk, and this hunger to be with You. To spend time speaking to You about birds in the trees, the fly on the windowsill, or a car passing by. To ask Your heart about items reported on the news, drinking in Your take on issues of life. To gasp in wonder at the glory of colours and to be lost in Your presence in the depths of songs, the beauty of music, and the glory of light.

I'm not sure if this communing link went back even before I consciously knew You—perhaps all the way back to those days when my spirit strummed and my lips hummed as I went about daily chores, so much so that a close friend nicknamed me the 'humming Pearlie Wearlie'.

Or perhaps it began when that gracious evangelist lady prayed over me at the outreach meeting all those years ago in Our Saviour's Church in Lagos. I still hear her words so clearly: 'O my Father, may prayer be as natural to this one as breathing.' My heart resonates with and echoes that prayer to this day.

Draw me deeper into You, dear Lord. Take me further than I've ever gone before. Father, I yearn for the intimacy cloaks, the presence ephods, and the fellowship mantles of the saints of old. So, Lord, I'm taking a deep breath. Take me deep diving with You. Take me to the place of Your deep presence, anointing, and glory. As the deer longs for the water, dear Lord, my soul longs for You.

> Deep calls to deep at the noise of your waterfalls: all your breakers and waves have swept over me. (Psalm 42:7 NKJV)

PRAYER INSPIRATION: A CONFESSION

> O Lord, take me deeper with You than I have ever gone before.

A HEART FOR GOD'S PRESENCE AS THE DEER PANTS

O Father, let this be my journey, my story, and my testimony.
This 'longing, thirsting, panting after You' chase …
Let it define me,
A visceral longing from deep within.
Lord, I pursue You,
Follow hard after You
Wholly and wholeheartedly.
Father, grant me Caleb's zeal, spirit, and focus.
Abba, draw me deeper in with You today and every day.

> To the Chief Musician. A Contemplation
> of the sons of Korah. As the deer pants for
> the water brooks, So pants my soul for You,
> O God. (Psalm 42:1 NKJV)

A psalm of David when he was in the wilderness of Judah.

> O God, You are my God; Early will I seek
> You; My soul thirsts for You; My flesh longs

for You In a dry and thirsty land Where there is no water. (Psalm 63:1 NKJV)

But my servant Caleb—this is a different story. He has a different spirit; he follows me passionately. I'll bring him into the land that he scouted and his children will inherit it. Hebron belongs to Caleb son of Jephunneh the Kenizzite still today, because he gave himself totally to God, the God of Israel. (Numbers 14:8–9, 14 NKJV)

Except for Caleb son of Jephunneh. He'll see it. I'll give him and his descendants the land he walked on because he was all for following God, heart and soul. (Deuteronomy 1:36 NKJV)

A HEART FULL OF PASSION

A fire on the inside, an ongoing passion:
A heart's cry to go higher up, further in; to travel to places ever deeper with my King.
Breath yielded, breath presented, breath submitted for conversion into prayers.

So breathe and pray, breathe and pray. A breath for a prayer:
Breathe, pray, breathe, pray, breathe, pray.

Breathe in … Lord, I love You.
Breathe out … Lord, I praise You.
Breathe in … Lord, I worship You.
Breathe out … Lord, I adore You.
O Lord, You are so very beautiful to me.

A breath and a prayer,
A breath and a prayer:
Lord, grant grace that the life of prayer becomes daily ever more natural to me.

> With all prayer and petition pray [with specific requests] at all times [on every

occasion and in every season] in the Spirit, and with this in view, stay alert with all perseverance and petition [interceding in prayer] for all God's people. (Ephesians 6:18–20 AMP)

PRAYER INSPIRATION: AN EXERCISE

Why not try making every breath a prayer for the next five or so minutes?

Breathe in …Lord, I love You.
Breathe out …Abba, I need You.

A HEART FULL
OF WORSHIP

*Of silent adoration, instrumental worship, and the talking
drum*

Abba Father, thank You for the places of silent adoration,
instrumental worship, and gently tinkling piano keys.

Thank You, Lord, for the bass guitar, the drums, the shaking
and jingle of the tambourine.

Because Lord, sometimes it's in the stillness,
And other times when the thunderous noise comes,
As the 'talking drum' begins to speak,
My heart indicts that noble theme
And starts reciting that composition to You, my King.

Adoring, worshipping, lifted, and exalted—
And suddenly,
I'm beholding beauty,
Bowing before majesty,
Amazed by glory,

Humbled by mercy,
Covered by grace,
Captivated by love.

In awe before the throne,
My Father's throne, and beckoned to come. Beckoned, not summoned;
Loved on, not commanded; gentled, not broken.
And like a flash, I'm up on my feet, like a small child heading for its daddy's arms.
I'm making that same darting run
Up the throne room steps and into waiting arms, eyes fixed on eyes filled with love.
Your lap my destination, Your chest my head's home, to lean on You,
Lean into You; in my Father's arms, I'm home.

Dear Lord, grant us grace that we make the journey from subject to loving daughter or son, Not losing one iota of the awe that is due Your name.

> My heart is overflowing with a good theme;
> I recite my composition concerning the King;
> My tongue is the pen of a ready writer.
> (Psalm 45:1 NKJV)

> One of His disciples, whom Jesus loved (esteemed), was leaning against Jesus' chest.
> (John 13:23 AMP)

PRAYER INSPIRATION: AN EXERCISE

Why not spend some time worshipping and praising Abba Father?

You can choose some hymns or instrumental worship, or if you prefer, play some songs of high praise.

A HEART FOR
THE ELDERLY

Abba Father, it is hard to watch my folks growing old. So hard to see the dad, whom I had to run after to keep up with as a child, need support to get to his bedroom door.

So hard to see the mum who could push a heavy buggy uphill to the train station (or hurl a cane at you from twenty paces) labour to step into a car.

It hurts to see these things, Lord.
Ageing is hard—hard to watch, hard to work through.
Scary, even.
And yet You said that even in ageing, You are there.

You are there, the ever-present companion,
The God who numbers every hair on our heads, numbers the grey and white ones too.
God to hoar hairs, God to grey hairs.
God from life's very beginning to its end.

God of all.

Lord of all, there is nothing too hard for You.

Be merciful to our folks as they age, O Lord. Show their loved ones grace in the ageing process too. Teach us care, tenderness, reverence, and respect. Dispel fear—fear of the elderly, fear for the elderly, and fear in the elderly too.

Because amid medical appointments, failing limbs, and sometimes even failing memories, there's promise in this season too. Promise that even to old age, You are still the same, unchangeable, with the same tenderness, the same affection, the same care for Your own.

God of infancy and childhood, I'm so grateful that You are also the Lord of old age.
You are ever faithful, never forsaking, carrying Your precious ones at every life stage.

O Lord be merciful to our folks as they age.

PRAYER INSPIRATION: A REFLECTION

Reflect on the scriptures below and ask the precious Holy Spirit to inspire your prayers.

> 'Listen to Me,' [says the Lord], 'O house
> of Jacob,
> And all the remnant of the house of Israel,
> You who have been carried by Me from
> your birth

And have been carried [in My arms] from
the womb,
Even to your old age I am He,
And even to your advanced old age I will
carry you!
I have made you, and I will carry you;
Be assured I will carry you and I will
save you.

O God, You have taught me from my
youth,
And I still declare Your wondrous works
and miraculous deeds.
And even when I am old and gray-headed,
O God, do not abandon me. (Psalm 71:17–
19 AMP)

For this God is our God for ever and ever:
he will be our guide even unto death.
(Psalm 48:14)

The righteous will flourish like the date
palm [long-lived, upright and useful];
They will grow like a cedar in Lebanon
[majestic and stable].
Planted in the house of the Lord,
They will flourish in the courts of our God.
[Growing in grace] they will still thrive and
bear fruit and prosper in old age;
They will flourish and be vital and fresh
[rich in trust and love and contentment];

[They are living memorials] to declare that the Lord is upright and faithful [to His promises];
He is my rock, and there is no unrighteousness in Him. (Psalm 92:12–15 AMP)

A HEART FOR THE YOUNG

(BLESS THIS CHILD)

Bless this child, O Lord.
And concerning them,
In Your mercy fulfil Your eternal plan,
That great and eternal purpose that You intended before
time began.

When gazing at unformed substance,
Light coming, forming, shaping,
You made
A unique and special bundle of joy.

Bless this child, O Lord,
This one You planted in a mother's womb
Father's reward
Brought forth on a day of heavenly joy.

Bless this child, O Lord.
Anointed, called, appointed,
Destined for greatness.

Make this one an arrow in Your hand,
A polished shaft,
A carrier of Your ordained praise,
A stiller of the enemy and avenger.

Father my Father,
Bless this child, O Lord.

> For You formed my inward parts; You covered me in my mother's womb.
> I will praise You, for I am fearfully and wonderfully made; Marvellous are Your works,
> And that my soul knows very well.
> My frame was not hidden from You, When I was made in secret,
> And skilfully wrought in the lowest parts of the earth.
> Your eyes saw my substance, being yet unformed.
> And in Your book they all were written,
> The days fashioned for me,
> When as yet there were none of them. (Psalm 139:13–16 NKJV)

> And the Child continued to grow and become strong, being filled with wisdom. And the grace of God was upon Him. (Luke 2:40 NKJV)

> For this child I prayed. (1 Sam 1:27–28 NKJV)

PRAYER INSPIRATION: AN EXERCISE

Take a few moments to think about children you know personally. Pray a blessing upon them today. Consider writing your prayer below.

A HEART FOR THE YOUNG

(OF KNIVES, GUNS, AND GANGS)

Lay down that knife,
Put down that gun.

O Abba Father, there's been another one—
Another stabbing,
Another shooting,
Another violent crime,

Another young man gone home before his time,
Another mother burying a loved son in his prime,
Another daddy's girl shot on the street in a drive-by.

Mercy, Lord Jesus.
It is my heart's cry.
May Your blood preserve their blood,
Save those appointed to die.

Have mercy, Lord.
Have mercy, my heart cries.

Have mercy, dear Lord.
Don't let another child die.

Father, I'm on my knees, crying out for mercy.

> If my people, which are called by my name,
> shall humble themselves, and pray, and
> seek my face, and turn from their wicked
> ways; then will I hear from heaven, and will
> forgive their sin, and will heal their land. (2
> Chronicles 7:14 NKJV)

PRAYER INSPIRATION: REFLECTION AND INTERCESSION

Take a few moments to think about a young person or
young people you know personally. Pray a blessing upon
them today.

How much do you know about gang warfare? Gun crime?
Pray for an end to violence and senseless killings.

Consider writing your prayer below.

A HEART FOR THE ALIEN
AND THE STRANGER

A tiny child washed up on an ocean shore …*
A frozen man falling from the sky …**
A mother and child clinging to a crowded lifeboat, inches away from a watery grave …***
A lorry load of women and children suffocating in a packaging container …****
And Lord, there are so many, many, many more.
The poor, the dispossessed, the displaced—desperate ones looking for a place to call home.

O Lord have mercy on the refugee, the outcast, on the alien and the stranger.

Did I hear someone say 'migrant', 'lesser life', 'just send them home'?

Surely there must be yet one more measure of grace, one more hand of kindness extended?

There must be a now response to your question from all those years ago, Lord. An answer to the question 'Who is my neighbour?'

Where is today's love and compassion-filled Samaritan, dear Lord?

And in the midst of the clamour …
Swirling in the political spaces.
Seeping around the edges of fears, immigration quotas, and every reason to simply look away …

Above the noise, Abba Father, I hear Your heartbeat,
And my heart beats in resonance with Yours.
I'm on my knees, Lord,
On my face interceding for the alien and the stranger.

Preserve their lives, Lord.
Raise up helpers, Lord.
Draw them to You, Lord.
Precious Father, bring them home.

> And if a stranger dwells with you in your land, you shall not mistreat him. The stranger who dwells among you shall be to you as [a]one born among you, and you shall love him as yourself; for you were strangers in the land of Egypt: I am the Lord your God. (Leviticus 19:33–34 NKJV)

The Parable of the Good Samaritan
And behold, a certain lawyer stood up and tested Him, saying, 'Teacher, what shall I do to inherit eternal life?'
He said to him, 'What is written in the law? What is your reading of it?'
So he answered and said, 'You shall love the Lord your God with all your heart, with all your soul, with all your strength, and with all your mind,' and 'your neighbour as yourself.' 'And He said to him, 'You have answered rightly; do this and you will live.' But he, wanting to justify himself, said to Jesus, 'And who is my neighbour?' (Luke 10:25–37 NKJV)

PRAYER INSPIRATION AND REFLECTION

*BBC Report: three-year-old child w*ashed up on a beach, 3/9/2015.
** *Mirror report*: *twenty-six-year-old man*, a stowaway from Angola, fell from a London-bound flight.
*** *Royal Mail Report: Woman and children* among 18,000 migrants rescued by navy from Mediterranean, January 2018
*****Telegraph report: driver jailed for fourteen years after deaths of fifty-eight Chinese* immigrants who suffocated in the back of a lorry as he tried to smuggle them into Britain, 6/4/2001.

Lord, who is my neighbour?

A HEART FOR THE BROKEN, THE DESPAIRING, AND THE DOWNCAST

Lord, You are close to the one whose heart is broken,
Close to the girl scoring her arm with nails,
Close to the young man slashing his wrists with glass.

Lord, You hear the soundless scream of the overwhelmed work colleague,
The desperate cry of the boss on the edge,
The heartfelt moan of the hopeless jobseeker,
The despair of those for whom it's all just become too much.

And all across life's battlefields, you listen in, Lord …

You listen in, O Lord, and You hear.
You listen in, O Lord, and You care.
Open my ears, Lord, to the cries of the desperate.
Break my heart, Lord, for what breaks Yours.

> The Lord is close to the broken hearted
> and saves those who are crushed in spirit.
> (Psalm 34:18 NKJV)

PRAYER INSPIRATION: AN EXERCISE

Can you identify any broken and downcast people in your sphere of influence? Why not pray for them today? Is the Lord asking you to do something about them?

A HEART FOR THE PERSECUTED CHURCH

Lord, my heart breaks when I see reports about churches
that have been blown up on the news.
It's so hard to see the tear-stained faces of brothers and
sisters,
The brokenness of ones who love You the way I do.
Hearts breaking and broken,
Loved ones lost,
Limbs and lives shattered,
Prices paid in lives marked by the cross.

Yet because of the cross,
The true price was paid
For humanity vile, wicked, and dark,
For a blaspheming world, tortured
And lost,
For ones destined to die without the man who died on the
cross.

And even so, Lord,
I recognise Your mercy

That I serve you in a nation
Where my local church isn't blown up,
Where I openly worship and call You Lord and Saviour,
Where my adoration has not been shut up.

And so, Lord, today I offer my devotion,
My prayers and intercession for ones paying that higher cost,
Where worship means imprisonment
And conversion means dying,
Where honouring your name
Means paying the ultimate cost.

Today, Father, touch me,
Move me,
Shake me.
Breathe through me sweet Spirit prayers that my persecuted
family needs.
May my intercession preserve them,
Strengthen and uphold them,
Until the day when we all meet at Your feet.

> Precious (important and no light matter)
> in the sight of the Lord is the death of
> His saints (His loving ones). (Psalm
> 116:15 AMP)

> His loved ones are very precious to him
> and he does not lightly let them die. (Psalm
> 116:15 TLB)

PRAYER INSPIRATION: REFLECTION AND INTERCESSION

The list below is compiled annually by Open Doors (https://www.opendoorsuk.org/), whose researchers assign a point value to incidents of persecution—forced conversions, attacks on churches, arrests, and more. Open Doors has published its list for twenty-six years.

Today, pray for persecuted brothers and sisters in these nations as the precious Holy Spirit leads.

The group's top ten countries where Christians face the most persecution are as follows.

- ❖ North Korea (94 points)—Christians and Christian missionaries are routinely imprisoned in labour camps.
- ❖ Afghanistan (93 points)—The government of this country does not recognise any of its citizens as Christian.
- ❖ Somalia (91 points)—The Catholic bishop of Mogadishu has described it as 'not possible' to be a Christian in Somalia.
- ❖ Sudan (87 points)—The government has slated Christian churches for demolition.
- ❖ Pakistan (86 points)—Christians sit on death row, facing charges of blasphemy.
- ❖ Eritrea (86 points)—Only four religions are officially recognised: Sunni Islam, the Eritrean Orthodox, Roman Catholic, and Evangelical Lutheran churches. Those belonging to other faiths

are persecuted, and those of recognised faiths are harassed by the government.

❖ Libya (86 points)—The government is reportedly training militants to attack Coptic Christians.

❖ Iraq (86 points)—Iraqi Christians have yet to return to their homelands after expulsion by ISIS.

❖ Yemen (85 points)—The ongoing political and humanitarian crisis has further squeezed Christians and other religious minorities, who already faced severe restrictions on practising their faiths.

❖ Iran (85 points)—Religious minorities, including Christians, face 'systematic, ongoing, and egregious violations of religious freedom' according to the US State Department.

A HEART FOR THE LOST

Father, thank You so very much for Jesus.
Thank You for the kind of love that paid the ultimate price,

A love that held nothing back.
Thank You for the value You place on every life.
Bought by blood and death on a Roman cross.
More precious than silver, gold, diamonds or rubies.
Because You loved You gave …

Lord, I'm so very grateful
That You saved me.
Through me now, Lord,
Touch and save ones who are lost.

> For God so loved the world that He have
> His only begotten Son that whosoever
> believes in Him should not perish but have
> everlastingly life. (John 3:16 NKJV)

PRAYER REFLECTION

Take some time to reflect on unsaved people in your sphere of influence; that may be family, friends, work colleagues, and others. Ask the Holy Spirit for whom you should pray. Ask if He has any other instructions for you to draw them to salvation in Jesus.

A HEART FOR THOSE IN AUTHORITY

Father, today I pray for leaders.
O Lord pour out fresh grace on the ones called to shepherd others.
Abba Father strengthen their hands.

Anoint them by Your Spirit, precious Lord, and grant them wisdom, insight, and discernment.

In a world scarred by conflicts, scarcity,
And complex challenges, grace them with heavenly wisdom to know what to do.

This very hour, Lord, I stand in the gap.
O Lord lift up the heads of your royal ones.
Fill their hearts with courage and deliver them from evil in Jesus's name.

> Therefore, I exhort first of all that supplications, prayers, intercessions, and giving of thanks be made for all men, for

kings and all who are in authority, that we may lead a quiet and peaceable life in all godliness and reverence. For this is good and acceptable in the sight of God our Saviour. (1 Timothy 2:2 NKJV)

PRAYER REFLECTION: AN EXERCISE

Have you prayed for the leaders you know today? Why not think of at least one leader now?

It may be someone you know at home, church, or work, or it may be a leader in your city or nation.

You may choose to record your prayers below.

PART TWO

A HEART INSPIRED

A HEART INSPIRED

Father, as I read the opening lines and first chapter of John Wimber's book *Prayer as Intimate Communication*, I found myself bowing my head and leaning upon the pages of the book, smelling its new book freshness and at the same time feeling like a parched one encountering a deep, refreshing draught of cool well water.

My soul drinks in afresh the deepest passion of my being to be intimate with my Father, to connect anew with the One who loves me deeply, the One my heart pursues to know and be known. Precious Abba Father, there is none like You. Draw me after You, and let us run together. As Enoch walked with You, so let me walk too.

Wrap me in the cloak of Your love, in the garment of Your presence. May I know you more and more. Surround me with Your presence, my Father and my God.

And Lord, in the pages of this book, my heart acknowledges the paradise that is intimacy with You regained.

As the deer pants for the water brooks, So pants my soul for You, O God.
My soul thirsts for God, for the living God. When shall I come and appear before God? Deep calls unto deep at the noise of Your waterfalls;
All Your waves and billows have gone over me. (Psalm 42:1–2, 7 NKJV)

HEART CRY

CRY:

Father, my family's safety and my own fruitfulness is in
Your hands.

I know that in my head. Deliver me from fear, Lord, that it
may rest in my heart.

It's time to move away from being managed, manipulated,
and controlled by my own fears, internal pressures; to make
decisions freely based on knowing that You love me and are
planning for me. Lord, I want a quality of peace and quiet
assurance in You in my mind, heart, and walk that I have
not experienced to date.

Precious Holy Spirit, I ask that you overshadow me, that
You fill me, and that You lead and guide me. This is a new
place for me, and I cannot walk it without You.

ABBA'S RESPONSE:

Daughter, you have cried out for My presence, and I will
answer and also pour My grace out upon you.

Your word for this year is grace.

In all things, I will show you My grace
Starting with your work—a role you were not looking for
and in the area of ministry.
Yes, even in the place of momentum, I will give you My
grace.
Do not be afraid.
My presence and My grace will be your shield and covering.

I've seen you labour as one breaking rocks in a quarry,
Serving in pain … I didn't call you to that and don't ask it
of you.
Now, receive My grace. Trust me.

I call you my beloved confidante.
Come back to My knee,
The place of intimacy, of heart rest
Place your head on My chest,
Under my chin.
Daughter come rest on Me,
Rest in Me.
I am not upset with you.
I am not disappointed in you.
Even in your weakness,
You are lovely to Me
I love you. I have loved you with everlasting love,
Drawn you with everlasting kindness.
I am for you more than you can understand.
I am with you and will be with you even to hoar hairs.
Do not be afraid.

> The LORD has appeared of old to me,
> saying, Yes, I have loved you with an

everlasting love: therefore with loving kindness have I drawn you. (Jeremiah 31:3 NKJV)

I am dark, but lovely, you daughters of Jerusalem, like Kedar's tents, like Solomon's curtains. (Song of Songs 1:5 NKJV)

FOR MY MUM

(REFLECTIONS SITTING BY MUM'S HOSPITAL BED)

Dear Lord,
It's me. Here for my mum.
Lord, Mum's hand is really shaky today, and it's got me
thinking …

As a child, when my hands shook,
Mum fed me.
When I made a mess,
Mum cleaned up after me.
When I didn't understand,
Mum painstakingly explained
And then celebrated when I got it.

As a child, mum understood
That I needed support,
Needed nurture, needed care, needed holding …

And now, precious Lord, even as time and circumstance
cause tables to turn,
Grace me to be there,
To nurture, to care.
Grace me to be there for Mum as she was there for me.

May I glorify You, Lord, as I honour my mum.

> 'Honour your father and mother' which is
> the first commandment with a promise.
> (Exodus 6:2 NKJV)

LORD OF WORK

(PRAYING AT MY DESK)

Grace me today as I work, O Lord.
Strengthen me to do Your will.
Bless me, Lord, as I work today.
May heaven's purpose be fulfilled.

Anoint me in my meetings, Lord.
Speak wisdom throughout my day.
Let my words and deeds honour You.
May my carriage Your nature portray.

Please help me as I work, O Lord.
Attune my ears and heart to Your voice.
Make me by Your hand, dear Lord,
Your ambassador of choice.

Through me bring in Your presence and glory.
Lord, may my workplace be transformed by Your grace.
Anxieties dispelled, oppressions overthrown, and
Breakthroughs the hallmark of this day.

O Lord of the diligent and the consistent,
Ruth's shield, Daniel's help, Joseph's companion,
Anoint and favour me as I work, O Lord,
Today and every day.

> And in all matters of wisdom and understanding, that the king enquired of them, he found them ten times better than all the magicians and astrologers that were in all his realm. (Daniel 1:20 NKJV)

> And the Lord was with Joseph. (Genesis 39:21-23 NKJV)

> As she got up to glean, Boaz gave orders to his men, 'Let her gather among the sheaves and don't reprimand her. Even pull out some stalks for her from the bundles and leave them for her to pick up, and don't rebuke her.' (Ruth 2:15–16 NKJV)

KEEP ME CHARGED, LORD

Inspired by 'What Are You Plugged Into', a YouVersion Bible devotion

Lord, I have so many chargers, battery packs, and cables,
Ready in an instant to keep my devices able.
Cables for my mobile and plugs for my tablet,
Plus backups for my backups—all keeping alive calls,
Twitter, and WhatsApp.

Lord, today I've been challenged about what keeps my life able.
Challenged about how I rate when it comes to spiritual battery chargers and cables.
How do I rate on those plugs, connectors, and links to You?
Do I take the same care to stay charged so You can get through?

Today, I ask for mercy, for grace and forgiveness too.
For a fresh hunger, new thirst and longing,
For a deeper yearning for You.

Grant me more passion for Your word and

Draw me by Your power
As a lighting cable to a source ...
Connect me with You this hour.

And as I connect,
O Mighty King,
Grant grace and keep me focused.
Charge me, Father, deep within.
May I never forget to plug myself in.

> For this reason I bow my knees before the
> Father, from whom every family in heaven
> and on earth is named, that according to
> the riches of his glory he may grant you
> to be strengthened with power through
> his Spirit in your inner being. (Ephesians
> 3:14–19 NKJV)

HELD IN YOUR ARMS

Thank You, precious Lord, for the assurance that You are in the midst of my life and circumstances, and that you quiet me with singing.

I am truly grateful for it. I love the picture and, even as I type this, the reality of You being my heavenly daddy. My beloved Abba Father, I'm so grateful that I'm held by You.

I truly thrilled that my entire family, everyone I love and all for whom I pray, comes under the canopy of Your gracious, loving, singing presence.

Held in Your arms, precious Father, we're home.

Hallelujah!

> The Lord your God in your midst, The Mighty One, will save; He will rejoice over you with gladness, He will quiet you with His love, He will rejoice over you with singing. (Zephaniah 3:17 NKJV)

PRESENT FATHER

Abba Father,
I rejoice that You are
God, who can't be contained by the heavens, and yet you
are so very present with me.

Present by Your Spirit, touching the depths of my heart.
Present hearing my cries,
Feeling my pains,
Multiplying my joys …

Present, so loving, caring, tender,
Even in this moment …
I can feel Your breath, precious Holy Spirit,
And I'm excited.
Draw me closer, Lord.
Come, precious Holy Spirit, and keep on coming.

INSPIRATION AND EXERCISE

Why not take a little time to sit a while with your loving
Abba Father?

Relax.

What is He saying to you?

Invite the precious Holy Spirit to speak.

You may want to write His words to you below.

THINKING OUT LOUD:
REMEMBERING A
DEAR FRIEND

Precious Abba Father, it's 31 December, and what a whirlwind year it's been. And so even as it draws to a close, Lord, receive thanks for Your faithfulness, Your mercy, Your many kindnesses, and Your hugely gentle care.

Thank You for everyone whom You brought alongside me this year; in Your compassion, bless and be gracious to them and accelerate them greatly in their destiny purposes.

Thank You for absent loved ones and especially for the witness, testimony, and inspiration of the wild and precious life of my friend Vicky Taylor.

Dear Father, so many of us love and miss her dearly. And in the very midst of heartache, Lord, we're truly grateful for the assurance that she's dancing with you, close to Your heart.

By Your grace and the power of Your Spirit, we pray and press on.

—December 2015

A HEART FULL OF PRAYERS-REPRISED MUSINGS

My heart is full of prayers,
Lord, yet sometimes I wonder if they count ...

Wonder if I'm praying right, Lord, or if I should just sit praying out.

And still I find my heart so very full of prayers, Lord, they constantly bubble up.

Long prayers,
Short prayers,
Desperate prayers,
Funny prayers,
Prayers rising to Your throne.

Passionate prayers,
Compassionate prayers,
Deeply intimate prayers

Connecting me with You, Lord,
Linking me to my true home.

My heart is full of prayers, Lord.
Over the years I've learned You hear
The cry of every child, Lord,
Every murmured, fevered prayer.

You hear the faltering words, Lord,
The urgent cry for help,
The shrieks of joy,
The moans of pain,
The heartfelt sighs and cares.

So I won't stop praying,
Can't stop praying,
Cos Abba Father, I know You're there.

You hear me and You answer me
And invite me to draw ever near.

My heart is full of prayers, Lord,
As natural as breathing is to me.
Thank You for the gift of prayer, Lord,
That golden thread between You and me.
Thank You for the gift of prayer, Lord,
That language from above.
I'm humbled by Your gift of prayer, Lord,
So once again, into Your presence
I run …

I love the Lord, because He hears my voice
and my supplications. (Psalm 116:1 NKJV)

Keep on praying. (Ephesians 6:18 NKJV)

Never stop praying. (Ephesians 6:18 CEV)

REFERENCE RESOURCES
FOR PRAYER

BOOKS

The Holy Bible
Praying The Bible, by Donald Whitney
The Kneeling Christian, by Anonymous
Praying Hyde, by John Nelson Hyde
Rees Howells Intercessor, by Norman Grubb
The Hour That Changes the World, by Dick Eastman
Love on Its Knees, by Dick Eastman
A Closer Walk, by Catherine Marshall
Whispers of His Power, by Amy Carmichael
Good Morning Holy Spirit, by Benny Hinn
Practising the Presence of God, by Brother Lawrence
Spoken Word, by Gerard Kelly
The Listening Ear, by Larry Lea
Learning the Joy of Prayer, by Larry Lea
Could You Not Tarry One Hour? by Larry Lea
FerVent, by Priscilla Shirer
Power of Praying Series, by Stormie Omartian
This Present Darkness, by Frank E. Peretti

Piercing the Darkness, by Frank E. Peretti
The Complete Works of E.M Bounds on Prayer, by EM Bounds
Too Busy Not to Pray, by Bill Hybels
Beginning to Pray, by Anthony Bloom
A Praying Life, by Paul Miller

RESOURCES

BKIM Prayer CD—Psalm 18

Truth Vine Music Singles and EP's
Yeshua Reigns
Take me Home
Adored

ABOUT THE AUTHOR

Pearl Moses is a worshipper and an intercessor whose passion for intimacy with the Lord is born out of her testimonies of His compassionate mercy. These testimonies include deliverance from the spirits of fear and rejection, as well as experiencing significant physical and emotional healing. Consequently, she is particularly moved to see abused and broken people made whole, restored to the image of Christ and fulfilling God's calling on their lives.

Her experience includes over fifteen years ministering to women and young people, and her creative gifts include inspirational coaching and writing. As a 'digital scribe', she is passionate to see social media channels won over and used effectively to promote the gospel of Jesus.

Pearl is an ordained pastor with Betty King International Ministries and Truth Vine Church. She is married and has one stepson. She is also a seasoned legal practitioner.